First published in paperback in 1981 by Eyre Methuen Ltd
Reprinted thirteen times 1981, 1982 (four times), 1983, 1984, 1985 (twice),
1986, 1987, 1989, 1990
This edition published 1991 by Mandarin Paperbacks
Michelin House, 81 Fulham Road, London SW3 6RB

Methuen and Mandarin are imprints of the Octopus Publishing Group
a division of Reed International Books

Copyright © 1981 Simon Bond

ISBN 0 7493 0834 6
A CIP catalogue record for this book is available from the British Library

by the same author
Unspeakable Acts
A Hundred and One More Uses of a Dead Cat
Odd Visions and Bizarre Sights
Success and How To Be One
Teddy
Uniformity
Stroked Through the Covers
Totally U.S.
Odd Dogs
Holy Unacceptable

Printed in Great Britain by St Edmundsbury Press Limited,
Bury St Edmunds, Suffolk

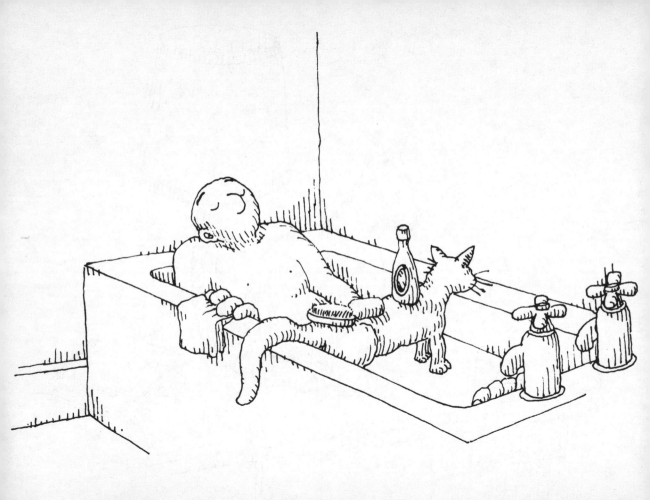

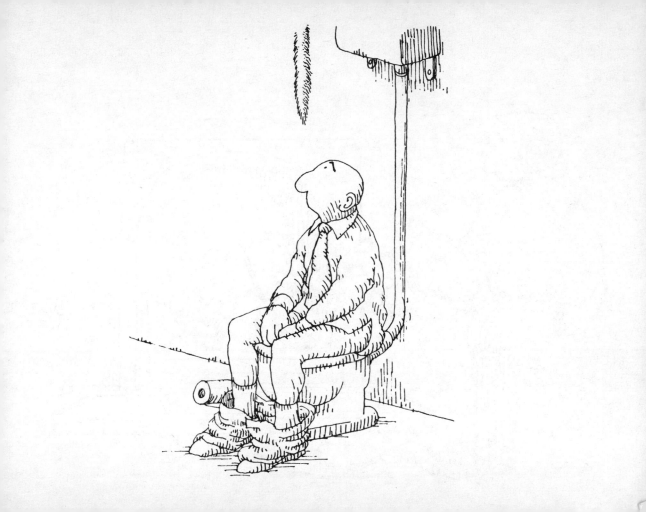

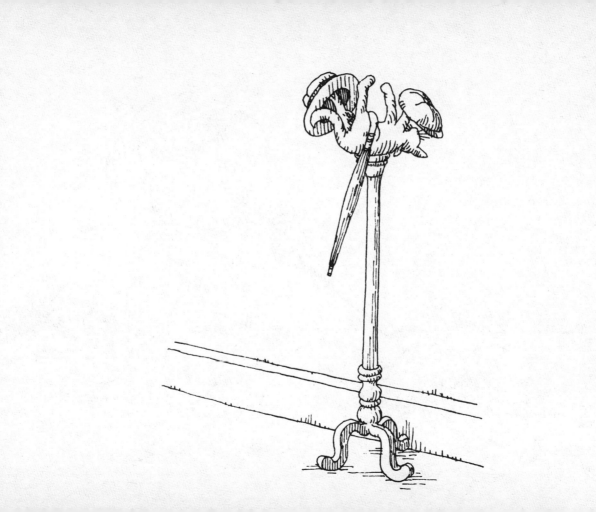

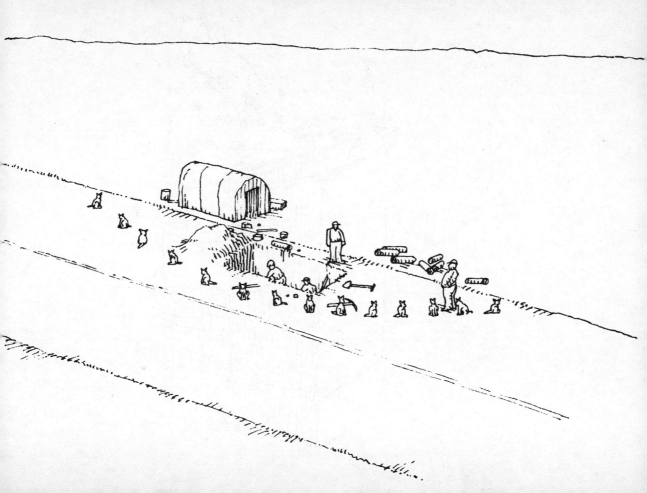

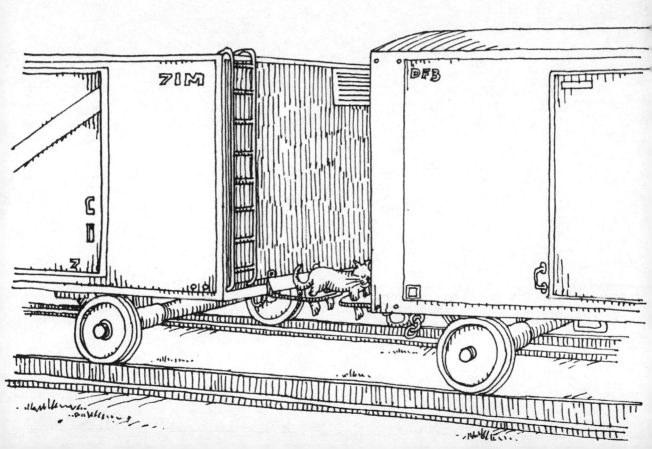

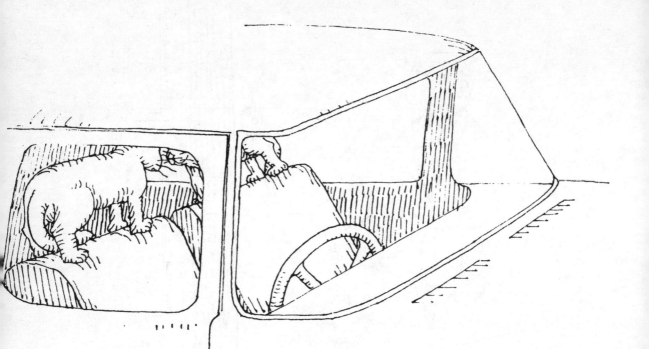

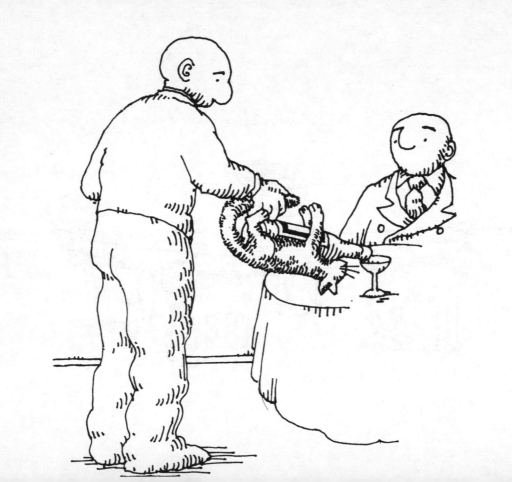

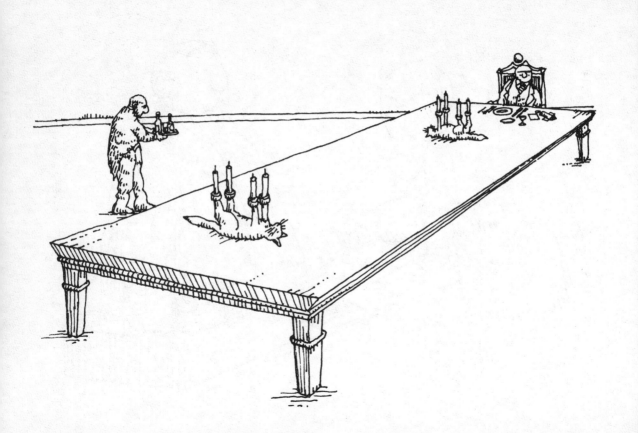

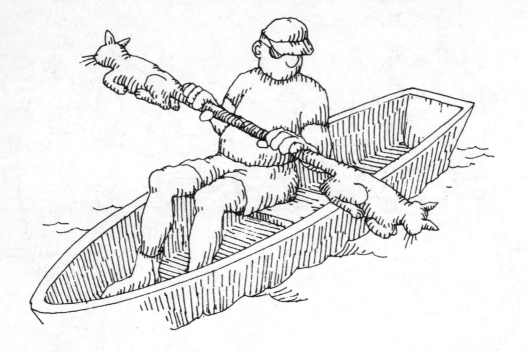

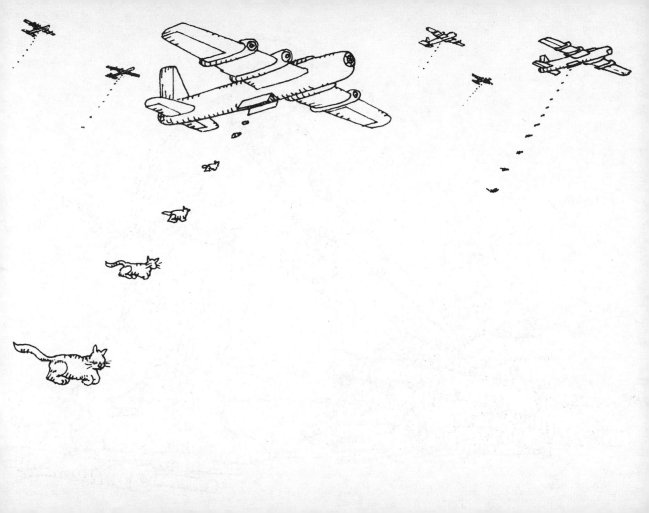

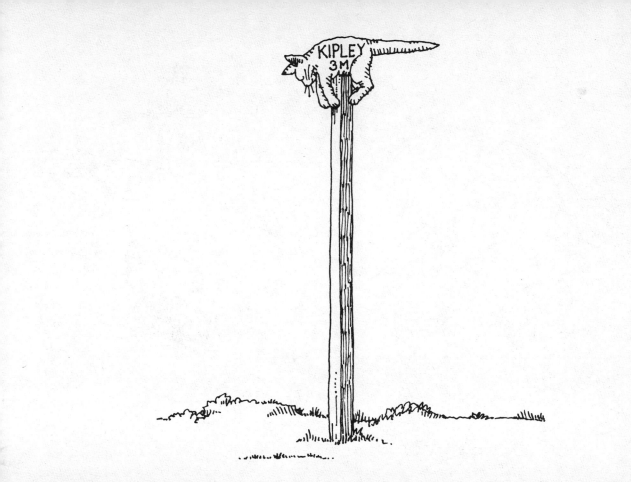

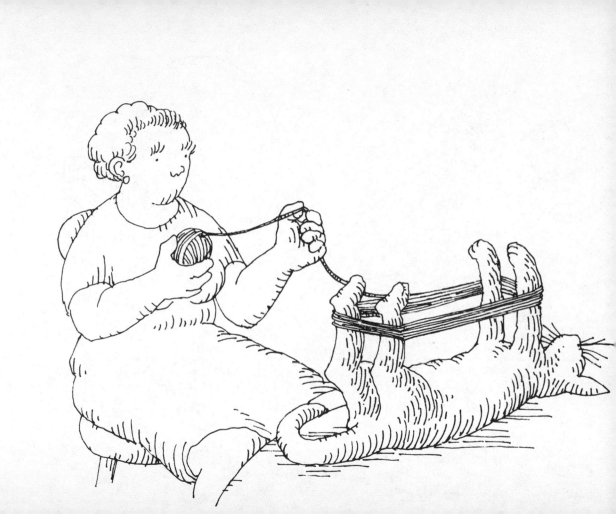

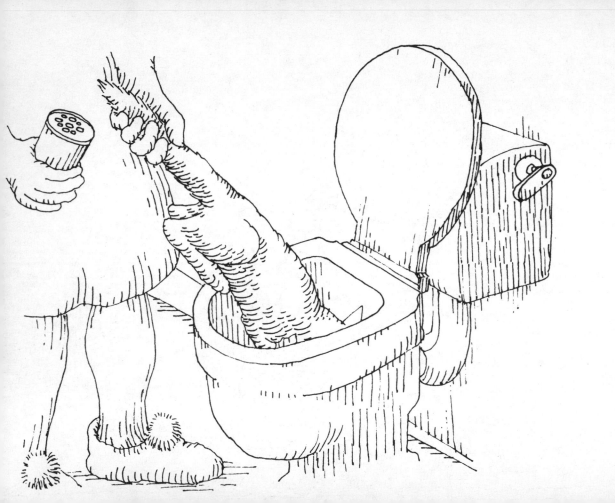

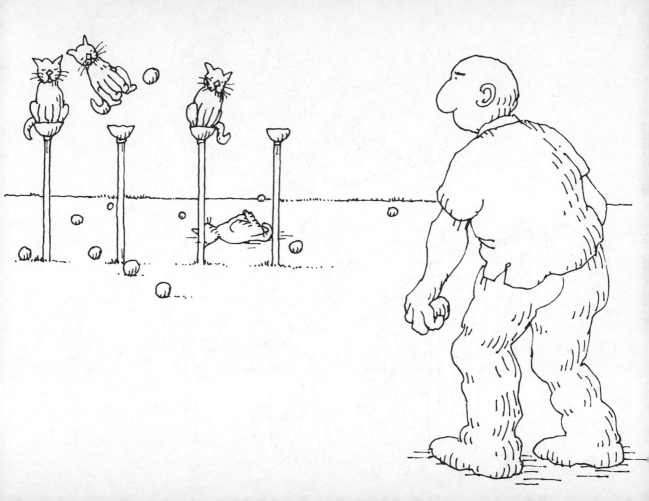

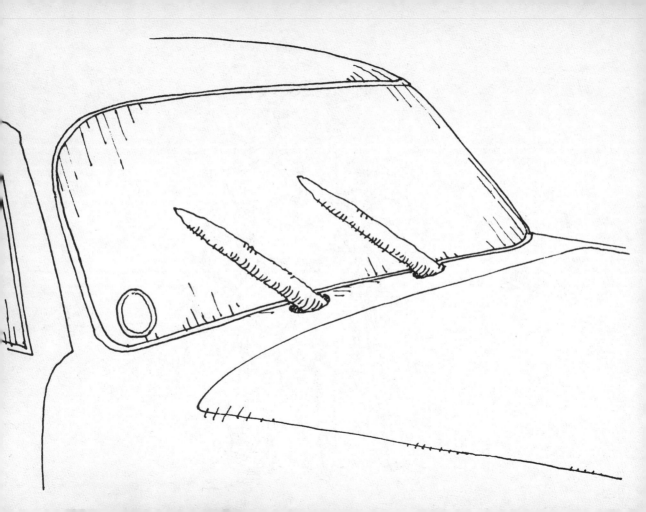

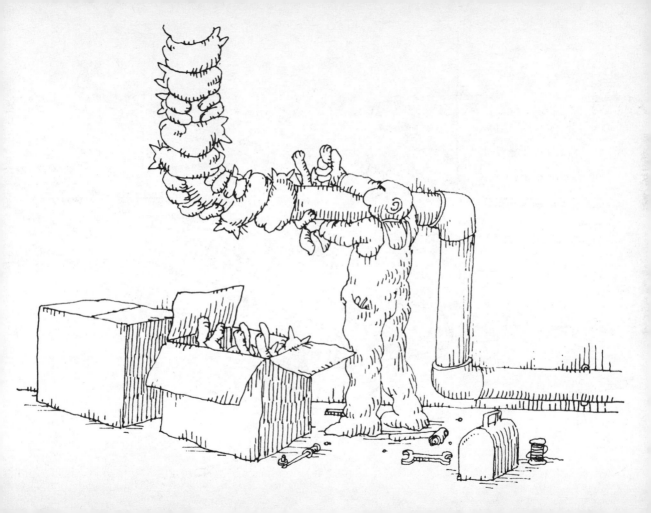

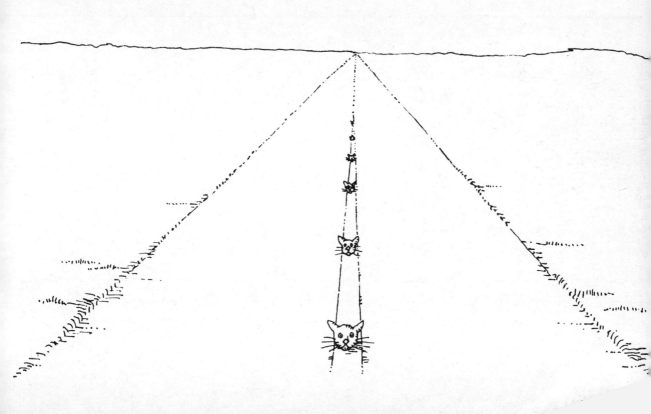